Can an ANT Carry Me?

Rourke
Publishing LLC
Vero Beach, Florida 32964

Meg Greve
and Jo Cleland

www.rourkepublishing.com

PHOTO CREDITS: © catman73: Cover; © Sergiy Available: Title Page; © Andre Armyagov, © David Hernandez: page 3; © Yuri Khristich: page 4; © James H. Carmichael: page 5; © Alex Wild: page 7, 9; © Andrey Pavlov: page 10; © Roger Milego: page 11, 13; © Mark Evans: page 14; © Jim Jurica: page 15; © Arlindo71: page 16; © Hung Meng Tan: page 17; © David Spieth: page 18; © Kathleen C. Petersen: page 19; © Darren Baker, Julie Ridge: page 20; © Jacom Stephens: page 21

Editor: Jeanne Sturm

Cover design by: Heather Botto

Interior design by: Renee Brady

Library of Congress Cataloging-in-Publication Data

Greve, Meg.
  Can an ant carry me? / Meg Greve and Jo Cleland.
    p. cm. -- (My first science library)
  ISBN 978-1-60472-536-0
  1.   Ants --Juvenile literature.
  QL568.F7 G74 2009
  595
                                      2008025158

Printed in the USA

CG/CG

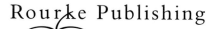

Rourke Publishing

www.rourkepublishing.com – rourke@rourkepublishing.com
Post Office Box 3328, Vero Beach, FL 32964

Ants are climbing up on me,

just as busy as can be.

Ants are black or brown,
or red, with three body parts –
abdomen, **thorax**, and head.

head

thorax

abdomen

5

Ants like drinking **honeydew**.

Other bugs taste yummy too.

7

Ants are working on six legs,

safely guarding **queen** ant's eggs.

8

Ants are very small, it's true.

So they share the tasks they do.

Thousands of ants all can squeeze,

into their homes called **colonies**.

Ants can lift things more than their weight,

even food right off your plate.

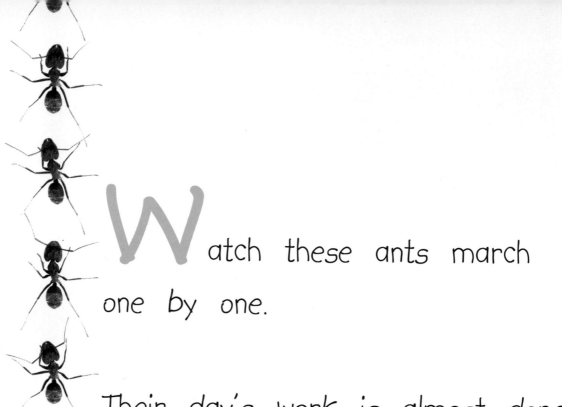

 atch these ants march one by one.

Their day's work is almost done.

16

17

Red ants bite and so do black.

Here's a warning, just stay back.

Ants are tiny, and as strong as can be. But they still can't carry me!

20

Glossary

abdomen (AB-duh-muhn): The abdomen is the big part of an ant's body that is like a stomach. You have an abdomen, too. It is the area of your body between your chest and hips.

colonies (KOL-uh-neez): Colonies are groups of ants living together. In an ant colony, different ants have different jobs to do.

honeydew (HUHN-ee-doo): Honeydew is a sweet juice that ants enjoy. Honeydew comes from aphids, tiny bugs that suck sap from plants.

queen (KWEEN): The queen ant is the mother ant for whom the other ants work. The queen lays all the eggs in an ant colony. Worker ants care for her young.

thorax (THOR-aks): The thorax is the part of an ant that is like its chest. It is the middle section of the ant's body.

Index

Further Reading

Dorros, Arthur. *Ant Cities*. Trophy Press, 1988.

Humphries, Tudor. *Are You an Ant?* Kingfisher, 2004.

Philpot, Lorna and Graham. *Amazing Anthony Ant*. Random House, 1994.

Websites

www.hello-world.com/English/song/ants.php

home.att.net/~B-P.TRUSCIO/STRANGER.htm

/ant.edb.miyakyo-u.ac.jp/INTRODUCTION/Gakken79E/Page_02.html

About the Authors

Jo Cleland loves to write books, compose songs, and make games. She loves to read, sing, and play games with children.

Meg Greve, an elementary teacher, lives in Chicago with her family. Currently, she is taking some time to enjoy being a mother and reading to her own children every day.